Lord
Dragonfly

William Heyen

Lord Dragonfly

Five Sequences

THE VANGUARD PRESS, INC.
NEW YORK

Library of Congress Catalogue Card Number: 80-28326
ISBN: 0-8149-0839-X (paper edition)
        0-8149-0853-3 (cloth edition)

Designer: Elizabeth Woll
Manufactured in the United States of America.

1 2 3 4 5 6 7 8 9 0

LIBRARY OF CONGRESS CATALOGING IN PUBLICATION DATA

Heyen, William, 1940 —
    Lord Dragonfly : five sequences.

    I. Title.
PS3558.E85L64   811'.54   80-28326
ISBN 0-8149-0853-5
ISBN 0-8149-0839-X (pbk.)

ACKNOWLEDGMENTS

The Ash appeared as a chapbook from Banjo Press in 1978. "The Eternal Ash" first appeared in *Skywriting*, "The Ash" in *Folio: Work in Progress*, edited by John Slathatos and Martin Booth (London: Oxus Press/Sceptre Press, 1977). "The Zenith Ash" first appeared as an *Ontario Review* postcard.

Lord Dragonfly was first published in *Poetry* and subsequently in a limited edition by Rook Press in 1978.

Abattoir Editions published *Of Palestine* in a limited edition in 1976. "Papyrus," "Watermelon," "Mustard," and "Anise" first appeared in *Poetry*.

XVII Machines was published in a limited edition by Rook Press in 1976. Some of its sections first appeared in *Beloit Poetry Journal, New York Quarterly, The New York Times, Review 74,* and *Thistle.*

Evening Dawning first appeared in a limited edition from William B. Ewert, Publisher, in 1979.

Contents

Lord Dragonfly consists of five sequences of poems written between 1974 and 1979. I've arranged the sequences here not chronologically, but in an order that itself forms, it seems to me, a sequence of sequences, each a consciousness defining its crises, straining to know, coming to something it can hold to. There is a clearing in the white space between sequences, but then a circling back, if obliquely, until, I hope, Lord Dragonfly sees from all sides at once.

W.H.

The Ash

The Ash

"Every minute, every day,
I hate this life.
I hate the trees, I hate the sunsets,
I hate my wife."

A nurse entered the room,
handed my friend his medicine,
a cup of water and two pills,
lithium and thorazine.

Eyes glazed, sedated,
but fists clenched above his sheets:
"I hate the doctors, the meals,
the beds, the stupid illiterates

who work here." I nodded,
but tried to save myself, ignored him,
closed my eyes, thought (for this was May)
of my mountain ash in white bloom,

at home, where I longed to be,
within its perfume-menstrual smell,
pure love mixed with death
mixed with pure swill

mixed with its own being
where, toward our earth's distillate,
airstreams of bees glide maddened
for blossoms of white filth,

thought of hands dipped
into cavities of ambergris,
of tongues licking scented necks,
lips sucking pus, maggots

humming their hymn of blue flame
in a dead animal's lung,
of the rainbow glaze of mucus,
the milky beauty of pond-scum,

of my own oval of flowering ash
in evening air, those powers that sustain
my body's sick-room odors,
the twisted smiles, the sunlit skin

cancers, the hate-vapors drifting
toward my broken friend, who cried
"I hate books, I hate the seasons,
I hate children, I hate the dead."

Where, if ever, will this end?
My friend moves from one ward to another,
embedded, circling lower. For now, outside,
I circle closer to the white ash flower.

The Ash: Its End

June, and gone is the flowering mountain ash's
too-full obscene odor,
with which I lived. Only thin perfume
lingers on the air

after its earthly love where
white blossoms have rusted:
tree at the end of something,
almost pure spirit at its end.

The Eternal Ash

By early August, the mountain ash's each limb
hangs heavy, its berry clusters
already tinged orange and bending its body
almost to breaking. The ash bears,

and will, this light, this weight.
Even at night under the frost stars, each berry
deepens into the ripe flame
autumn means for it to be,

yes, but to know one thing, but know it:
the lord of the whole tree, in time,
unchanged, its changes mine, delusion;
knowing, now, the mystical winter blossom . . . .

Which August is this, anyway? — this windless
poise of clusters that never fall, but will,
within the living tree that withers, while
ashlight drifts to the earth, petal by petal.

✻ The Flowering Mountain Ash Berry

Sperm floating in air,
  the earth to be its bed,
    packed in wet orange flesh,
      one luminous oval seed.

The Zenith Ash

September winds are elsewhere, have missed her.
Now the green oval of the flowering ash flames.
If I do not take her now,
while berry-clusters hemorrhage her limbs . . .

She is the holiness begun with one seed,
Yours, my Lord. Your
summer has burnished her branches
to this brown-black shine. Her

body does not wait. Time
is. If I, in human error, lose her,
even You, my Lord, will curse me:
each seed in each berry a skull's leer.

Now the green oval of the flowering tree
flames. And You are the slanting cancerous rays
of autumn sunlight, and You
the source that takes me, and this my ash of praise.

The Friend

Winter. My friend is not my friend,
probably will not return, raves and drools
oblivious to me, the doctors, the walls,
stares into a labyrinth's dead end

where history and logic die:
"I hate the chairs, the words,
the winds, the bastards
in bed with me all night."

But this time, home again
from visiting him, I stepped
from my car onto the shocked bone
of my body, and walked

into the snow-sheathed tree. No gloves
to touch it, I touched it, caressed it.
Flesh burned into its silhouette,
froze: held fast, I wept in waves

until I heard, at last, the lost man's song:
Goodby, friend, let me be alone.
Goodby, your body is a wing
as frail as mine.

Alive in its dumb sticks, the tree
flared, ice-white as stars. And You, Lord,
saw, had given me back to myself to see,

to say goodby to my dead friend,
and to love the dead.

Lord Dragonfly

i.

A friend dies.
Another,
forcing the lilac to flower.

ii.

In a corner of the field, wild
grapevine climbs a lightning
groove in the ash trunk.
Where are the dead?

iii.

In the field's drizzle and gloom,
soft-glowing sheaths,
the souls of spikes
of goldenrod.

iv.

Breaking the field I find
a ring of round white stones,
gift of the glacier.

v.

As I dig, the old apple stump
tries pulling itself deeper
by its last root.

vi.

Inside the windfall apple
tunnels of bees
singing.

vii.

I'm glad,
grasshopper of my childhood,
you've grown your legs back.

viii.

Pure white found
a wild rose to live in,
for now.

ix.

Half the mantis still
prays on my scythe blade.

x.

In the mowed field,
a million crickets for hire.
My steps are money.

xi.

My wife away.
In a garden furrow,
I find her lost earring.

xii.

Lord Dragonfly
sees me from all sides
at once.

xiii.

Pear blossoms
sift the same air
as last year.

xiv.

No one has ever
seen snow fall here,
until next year.

xv.

The hummingbird whirrs,
only its ruby
throat feathers clear.

xvi.

Curves of the summer pepper
lit with every green.

xvii.

With trees overhead,
where is the void?

xviii.

One red cardinal,
one gray cardinal,
three cinnamon-spotted eggs.

xix.

I am safe here,
not a friend in sight.

xx.

I lean on my shovel,
trusting the field.

xxi.

Playing dead,
Japanese beetles tumble
from a skeleton leaf.

xxii.

Already morning glory
tendrils circle
my shovel's handle.

xxiii.

Beneath its tassels
an ear of corn
erupts in fungus,
the blackest light.

xxiv.

When I look for him,
he is away,
finding another home,
the borer that killed my poplar.

xxv.

Prune for shade.

xxvi.

Rooted,
the trees are green islands
in fog
in the shifting field.

xxvii.

Sunflower, my lamp,
on such a rainy day.

xxviii.

Tree-man
carrying branches
of silver maple
I walk through the storm.

xxix.

Evening: time to level
the frantic anthill,
the field's brain.

xxx.

Meteor shower —
a little more, or less,
of the Lord.

xxxi.

Outside at night
I close my eyes:
the lost chestnuts' roots
luminous underground.

xxxii.

This western corner of the field,
this grove of ash —
if there were a place . . .

xxxiii.

Beetle's cargo:
heaviness?
happiness?
Neither, nor
both together.

xxxiv.

In the far galaxies,
collapsed stars,
yes, but here,
light escapes
even the blackberries.

xxxv.

In the autumn field,
my body,
a warm stone.

xxxvi.

Cosmos, planet, field,
and the dead
aware of everything!

Of Palestine

Almond

Palestine turns again to the year's first days.
Now, the almond bursts its head
into white and airy blossom.

What is this speech spoken in the wind,
in the bloom of the almond's white air?
What should we know of the blood's winter?

Old Arab, old Jew, or tree that you are,
snow-white January almond,
we can almost hear.

Papyrus

Once abundant, now rare,
growing almost in water, or in water,
its pith cut into strips and layered,
it was this that held the words.

Triangular stem, slender
leaves tufting ten feet above the marsh,
it was this that held the words,
the words of sunlight, or words

spoken, or breathed, or dreamed,
or gotten down on it with reed pens,
with soot and gum-thickened water.
It was papyrus held the words.

We could listen as it swayed in wind
above the sounds of water,
speaking with words of water,
the words of sunlight in its leaves.

✓ *Lily of the Field*

Consider them, said Jesus,
how they grow and do not toil,
nor spin. But even Solomon,
in all his glory,
was not arrayed like one.

We have seen them in their lids
of scarlet-red; but sometimes
white in Galilee, or on
the Plain of Sharon; but sometimes
Jaffa fields blow pale
blue with their delicate lashes.

Stem of tiny nerves
braided, six petals
Solomon's royal color,
and pupil of black seeds —
all pressed here
into our book as its eye.

Madonna Flower

No scripture names it.
The name for it came later.
Still, she would have seen it,
Mary, the mother its name remembers.
She would have seen it,
in Nazareth, and known it,
as other mothers, Arab and Jew,
still know it,

its white petals and feathery leaves —
we will place it
in clay bowls for their tables,
or on the fresh graves
of their friends, or, when time weaves,
as it will, again, as it has,
over their abdomens that swell,
under their hearts that grieve.

5

Passion Everlasting

Palestine remembers.
They were tipped red before.
And such a deep red suddenly to issue
from stems gray-white as ghosts.

They were tipped red before:
the flowing bodies of believers, disbelievers.
They have held buds of blood
above the ground as though the whole earth

were straining to bear the young men up
as do the weeping women
of so many paintings. Palestine
remembers: flowers for all passions everlasting.

3

4

Pheasant's Eye

Or called Adonis,
another flower to remember losses,
drops of blood. That handsome lad
is dead. In Palestine, the young men
still are dying. Their eyes shine
and weep red droplets to the grasses.
Next spring, Adonis blooms again.

Watermelon

The dry soil itself,
the sandy soil itself —
this is the temple, this
the miraculous dark mosque
of the melon placed
in Palestine for our tongues
to taste, to which we listen:

O Lords, your vines
are the melon's springs and rivers.
Allah, Jehovah,
what speech is this?
what words are these
that pulse fruit
from among the leaves, these

vowels intoning
low sounds in the wind, these
hard-skinned tear-
shaped melons, these
dusty gourds our thumbs
touch to glistening
greens and yellows?

Bean

Kneel with us, now,
within the ruins the Arabs call Chartula,
a hilltop where Joshua
commanded the sun and moon: *Stand still!*

Look down with us, now,
through the pass through the mountains
through the sacred land:
O Jerusalem.

The plant we will taste is tender,
but has survived,
leaves and tendrils multitudinous
as Allah's eyes,

its blossoms yellow
with a few dark stripes,
the Jew's star,
or his coat.

There is not yet
an ending to this.
The truth harbors
the bean's vine twisting

into thick matting
above the rich soil of ruins.
Allah, Jehovah, we taste
bitter love but pray for peace.

Mustard

Down at the lake we looked about us,
saw tares growing among the wheat,
saw fishermen at their nets,
saw the mustard's yellow blossoms,
pods bursting at the ends of stiff stems.

In dry graves its seeds have passed
millennia like minutes. Brought to light again,
these sprout in new tears. Tares, wheat,
fishermen still at their nets
under the golden sun, and mustard, for us

to taste the world's sorrow never grown old,
wisdom powdered to bloom on the tongue.

Cyclamen

Cyclamen aleppicum,
one of spring's first flowers,
unaware of its own Latin, so common is it,
so little does it need a name
to give its own sweetness to the air,

needing only mountains,
only its own blossoms of several colors
from pure white to spotted lavenders,
only the water its roots can kiss,
and April's gentle beginning flames.

Flax

In Egypt, in Palestine, flax
woven to linen wrapped
the dead.

Beige, cream, brown, white linen, but
nothing of the lavender flax
blossom that lights

whole hills in the living distance, not a word
of the slightest mauve speaks
from the linen,

and if death is as colorless as this, if
the Bible is wrong and the Koran
wrong and the Talmud

wrong that say those judged when that day
patterns the woof and warp, those
"companions of the right hand"

shall live forever with their Lord —
if the holy writings
are wrong,

if it is true that death is the beige, cream,
brown, white weave of flax,
if this is true . . .

Cedar

To lie down
    to sleep in the last grove
        of these oldest mothers

to breathe the resinous
    balsamic odors
        leaf and bole

to dream to fall
    from time to die
        to lose yourself

under evergreen air
    roots your pillow
        bark your hair

above you the earth's
    slight curve the trees'
        conical heads the sky's

blue-black dome
    how have you fallen
        this far

O death
    in whose wood
        our world is tongue

we cannot hear
    and what will save us
        when will we awaken

Lentil

What is the lentil's propaganda?
Which is its flag?

For beauty, for speech:
its pink tongues.

What is its passion?
Whose holy books burn
blood-red behind its million eyes?

For constant miracle, the lentil takes
to poorest soil, yields
fragrant pottage.

As the cities die,
and the people die? . . .

For the end of the world,
for after the end, the lentil.

Palm

One:
one
hundred
feet high:
taller than
idols, and alive,
wide leaves waving
over its knotted
trunk,
dates
in fifteen-
pound
clusters,
fruit
whose stones
we feed
to camels,
or mash for human
medicine.
We cut the tree
for baskets,
bags,
mats,
brushes;
for fences,
poultry
cages;
for thread,
ropes,
rigging;

for sap
liquor;
for thatch
shelter;
for fuel;
for wreaths
of honor;
for cover
for corpses;
for images
of conduct
in the wind,
tree never
aspiring
to heaven,
living
itself
in its own heaven
as the planet
circles,
as the galaxy
drifts
to nowhere we
will ever know,
this vertical
numinous
whip, this
shapeshifting
shade, this
palm

rooted
one
hundred
feet
deep
in our only
holiness,
soul,
earth's
sand,
soil,
rock.

Grass

"All flesh is as grass," said Peter,
    "but the word of the Lord endureth. . . ."
We have pressed wordless grasses into pages.
    Our flesh is in the grasses.

Anise

These are the last words of this, our prayer
to enter the anise yellow as sunlight,

to sleep in the shade
of the fig's five-lobed leaves,

in the calm of the cedar's horizontal branches,
to be dazed into rest by the mandrake's

magical human root, to dream
in medicinal anise light,

in the light of the leek's
invisible distillate,

of this land, this power, this
bulb, this Palestine broken open

under eyes that film with it,
and fill with tears.

XVII Machines

Machines To Kiss You Goodnight

Under the world's mountains
fossils tell the old story:
coal flowers shine
in their own black light.

Machines, rooted in bedrock,
question and answer themselves, recall
their dreams of numbers,
the sweet possibilities of fire.

Rockets hiss as though praying
for release, for the long arc under the sun,
then to tongue the earth again,
to kiss you, to flame.

✳ *The Machine That Kills Cats*

In an advanced technological society
the licensing of machinery
is the sole province of the state,
forever inviolate,

except for the patriotic few eccentric
sometimes angry inventive mechanics
and scientists whose daily food
is also the bread of common good,

and therefore I have sailed the seas
in full knowledge to please
those like myself who favor rats
and birds, and hate cats.

As a first gift to men
I built my machine
to hound them in their dark alleys,
or among vines and lilies,

where it clamps its iron jaws
on their backs, claws
their green eyes out with steel wires,
and sets them afire

until they burn to black dust.
My machine is the first
of many such whose one thought
is to track and kill the cat.

3
✴ *The Machine That Collects Butterflies*

Today is a lepidopterist's delight:
monarchs, swallowtails, rare finchwings
flutter and gambol in the meadow like lambs;
zephyrs bend the long grasses to waves.

Moving on a soft rush of air,
following your eye that follows
the single elusive butterfly
you've been searching for for so long,

the machine whispers a fine spray
that rainbows in the gold light,
brings your prize down to your feet
like a leaf: dead, beautiful,

and perfect, even the dust on its wings
shining for years in your glass box.

✴ *The Master*

Chess is not poetry, chess
is mathematics to the nth.
Track the master to his fifth move.
He'll track you to your tenth.

The steel trap of his mind:
sixty-four squares to shut upon.
This is the prose of iron,
not the poetry of winds,

fluids, curves, breaks, bends,
accidents or passions.
His moves are instant.
Your game ends

on a feudal rack
black and painful as the plague:
his queen, the spider of her several corridors,
and yours; his bishops,

the sole power of their diagonals;
his knights at your throat
with the jagged L's
of their axes. And as you die,

because his world was never
in doubt, never more secure,
his king sleeps a dreamless sleep
behind the stone towers of the royal bower.

The Line

The belt, a metal river, runs
its mile-long gauntlet of machines
bending above it like its mother,
goddess of hammers and shears.

O, lovely mother
of aluminum and oil,
mane of levers
and eyes of wheel,

fingers of knives
and kiss of laser,
breath of fume,
embrace of wire,

build slowly while I sing this song.
Because our lives are flesh, and short.
Because your art is longer, your
boys of piston, girls of gear.

*The Machine That Mends Birds' Nests

It's on its own, dispossessed,
day and night treads streets,
fields, corridors of buildings,
and the deep woods.

For somewhere a loose shoelace
threatens a child, a beam rots,
broken bottles need sweeping,
ice cracks a sidewalk, a cat

cries from a closet, ivy chokes
saplings, or a circuit shorts.
It's on its own now, its metal heart
obsessed with perfection.

A nest endangers its eggs:
even the oblivious robins blink
as this machine reaches up to bend
a twig here, to replace a grassblade, there.

The Machine That Air-Conditions The World

The Congo's hippo, the Nile's
cloudy myth-of-a-blue riverhorse who
all day chewed his cud
of lily-pads, who
all day drowsed in mud,
dreaming of flight while birds
pecked and danced his head,
now tiptoes
and cavorts the brush,
his whole being fluttering like flamingos.
On occasion, even Libya snows.

Now that the earth's one
air-conditioned hippodrome,
now that M.I.T.'s machine
monitors the world and beams
its cool breath over to Boston
or across the oceans,
now that the deserts' hot winds
and sandstorms are only the Bedouins'
old tales or, once in a while, someone's
sweaty dream, all our lives are lived
in the here and now, in one constant season.

The Machine That Treats Other Machines

This one, the most human,
can kill, has hands
that can crush gears, tubes,
tapes, parts beyond redemption.

This one is sure of itself as God.
When it destroys, it destroys;
when it repairs, its long and triple-
jointed touch is deft as a surgeon's.

Another machine sleeps at its switch:
this one embraces its ill brother,
dismantles, or cures. Impossible,
but no man told or tells it which.

✳ *One Machine's Perversity*

It could never get things right.
No means or machinations
could straighten it out.
Drank its instructions

like booze, sliced saplings in half
but spared the vines that choked them,
watered thistles and yanked roses,
mowed fields of green corn,

sprayed houseplants with oily urine,
killed, so to speak, the hounds,
and fed the rabid fox, an ox
lumbering clumsy the world's china shop.

When, at last, history's greatest lemon
ran down, we placed it in a zoo,
behind glass. Science is still lost
to know what told it what to do.

✳ The Machine That Balances Your Mood

Your guts tighten,
your brainwaves say
murder:
the machine's sensors
pulse, its face-plate
cracks a metal smile
like a damned fool,
a rusty comedian,
a mess of comic bolts, until
your red mood passes.

Or you say,
the hell with it all
and rush toward hell,
drain a bottle
of bad wine
by nine in the morning:
the machine steps up,
a Prussian officer,
shouts for order, becomes
your new drummer.

Or you're so
unreasonably happy
you can bless death
and wish to die:
the machine
clanks up,
moves to an oil and whirr
of tragic arrangement,
restores you
to a luke-warm world.

Now, at night,
as you walk from steady
shadows of trees held steady
in the steady
air, cricketsong
twirps along your nerves,
small acceptable scrapes,
while each star completes the scene,
ganglia and neuron,
of a friendly constellation.

✳ *The Companion Machine*

It toasts and butters,
watches you scan the morning papers, asks:
What do you think of those damned Chinese?
Did you see the report on the blue robins?

Your answers etched on its inner ears,
it nods, checks the barometer back of its head,
gathers your hat, umbrella and rubbers,
washes the dishes and makes your bed,

tells you how well you look today, o-
pens your door and walks you out: O
smell the rainy air today,
and wipe your rainy eyes, O

and kiss your machine goodby today,
and kiss your machine goodby. O.

*The Machine As Jewish Mother

She knows you're tired, hungry,
down to your last few coins.
She murmurs and prepares.

Her eyes light up. Her breath
steams like a cup of soup.
You whisper thanks and drink

the broth of her breasts, and chew
bits of chicken,
whole again, beyond confusion.

13

The Machine That Kisses You Goodnight

It runs on oil scented to pine.
Its shadow is a canopy of leaves.
Its gears mesh like grass.
It does not streak linen with grease.

It stands by your bed, a tree
of lights glowing soft as orchids
in the dark. It purrs and whispers
sleep, my pretty one, sleep.

After it reaches down, like the rain,
to kiss you, you'll dream all night:
bending above you, your metal mother
keeps you from harm. Sleep. Dream.

✳ *The Wedding*

After its great hands have held
the two of you in the one chapel
of its cupped palms
for a time you've lost all track of —

after the soundless music
of your loved one's love
has reached you
deeper than hearing —

after each of you is placed lost
and alone in the far valleys
of dark and are found again
to die together in satin —

after you break fast
with wine and flowers
and the words are told you
from the beginning —

you will walk out.
You will kneel in the shadow of its arms.
You will give thanks.
You will know you are wed.

✶The Machine In Your Field

Its fingers caress your chest
and reach in, pull out your heart.
And so on — liver, kidneys, teeth, lungs,
anything old, or diseased.

It lops off your legs and arms,
lifts your trunk, a cutting,
above the rich loam.
It plants you, heaps earth

in a mound around your neck.
You'll dry and dream in its rays.
The machine's gentle rain will bless you.
At night its own stars will burn above you,

its moon draw blood from your bones.
You'll stretch and grow, your shoulders
will break earth. The machine will lift you,
kiss your forehead, teach you to live again.

* This Hydraulic

This hydraulic lifts
your dark lungs and soul
toward the sun
in a glass bubble, a cell
of ease and sweet scents
that will never burst.

This hydraulic's steel shaft
bends in the wind
like a long-stemmed rose.
This hydraulic sways,
in mild and lemon light,
above the clouds.

You'll sleep and dream, sunlight will flower your bed of wires
to a tangle of tendrils,
until you'll awaken,
again a child, again
and again a child.

✳ *The Machine That Puts You To Sleep*

There does come a time,
after your several new lives,
to die. Your soul knows when,
and tells you, sometimes trembles
under a warm sun,
sometimes warms your limbs and face
in a flurry of snow
as though your bones were candles.
You know, and by this time
welcome your own soul's choice.
Those around you,
all those you've loved
for so long, will watch your eyes
begin to bloom to black flowers,
and will know, and be happy,
looking ahead to their own time.

Your soul will tell you the morning.
Your loved ones will walk you
to the machine's door, say
a few words, and walk away.
You'll enter the machine,
walk in the dark to where
a wall of water glows
with its own black light.
You'll walk into the water.
Your lungs will breathe water.
The water will lift you to where
your lives will pass before you
like a film. Now the machine's tides
will turn in deep silence. Now,
as though the moon drew you,
downward, the machine will drop you
into a dreamless sleep at last, forever.

Evening Dawning

i.

A crow's black squawk —
my white field lost again.

ii.

All bone,
feet numb,
rhythm gone,
I clod across the field.

iii.

From the outer world,
a siren, and a dog's
painsong.

iv.

In high snow,
which way the root,
which way the tip
of the bramble arch?

v.

Sparrow hearts
criss-crossing
the frozen field.

vi.

In the long, lowest needles
of white pine,
a message,
frozen in urine.

vii.

White moon shell,
and a single gull
flying toward me
from shore.

viii.

Upswirl, sudden
white-out.
My cabin within,
I close my eyes to find it.

ix.

My footprints already
in front of me,
I walk toward the other world.

x.

Bowing,
I address the door,
pray, once more,
for that opening
to everywhere,
and enter.

xi.

Pine chair cold,
hands cold,
mind cold
and ready.

xii.

World, mind, words —
wax, wick, matches.

xiii.

Under my cabin,
field mice,
and China.

xiv.

To see the white sea,
I and my old pen knife
scrape a porthole
in the frosted window.

xv.

Rabbit tracks,
rabbit pellets,
my own footsteps
drifting with snow.

xvi.

What kind of blood
in the red-twig dogwood?

xvii.

They disappear,
St. Francis now a spruce
receiving sparrows
into his dark boughs.

xviii.

Logic, logic —
trillions of intricate hexagons.

xix.

From another time
at field's edge
the first ash
veiled in a dream
in falling snow.

xx.

Cardinal,
mote of male blood
in the winter ash.

xxi.

Under the snow,
infinitesimal pearls,
insects speeding
to summer.

xxii.

Already ferns
frost my window.

xxiii.

I am thirty-eight.
Evening is dawning.

xxiv.

Lord, winter,
I place this cabin
in your begging bowl.

xxv.

Dying, the brain
sheds cells.
In the end,
perfect numbers,
the mind,
the Milky Way's stars.

xxvi.

Candlebeam and dust,
river and fish,
as long as they last.

xxvii.

Blue stars in the blue snow
over the elm stump.

xxviii.

In the window,
holding out their pale arms,
my mother and father,
above, within, beyond the field.

xxix.

I have come to have
everything, but now
the miserable
weep in chapels
under the spruce boughs.

xxx.

Even winter evenings
spores of black knot, killer
of cherry, plum, and apple.

xxxi.

mindless, invisible,
drift over the field,
but will anchor.

xxxii.

Verdun, Belsen, Jonestown — still,
from indwelling darkness, human
music, a summons
to praise.

xxxiii.

A boy, I killed these sparrows
whose *tsweet, tsweet* now
enters my cabin,
forgiving everything.

xxxiv.

I still hear
the summer woodpecker, red
godhead hammering holes
into my heartwood.

xxxv.

How long have I been here,
scent of pinesap
flowing through my chair?

xxxvi.

Snow clouds,
Milky Way nowhere in sight,
moon hidden, all
earth gone —
there is a life, this one,
beyond the body.

A NOTE ON THE AUTHOR

William Heyen was born on November 1, 1940, in Brooklyn, New York, and raised on Long Island. He received his Ph.D. from Ohio University in 1967, spent 1971–72 in Europe as a Senior Fulbright Lecturer in American literature, and now teaches at his undergraduate alma mater, the State University of New York College at Brockport. He edited *A Profile of Theodore Roethke* (1971) and *American Poets in 1976* (1976). *Lord Dragonfly* is his fifth full-length book of poems. His recent honors include the annual *Ontario Review* poetry prize (1977), the Eunice Tietjens Memorial Prize from *Poetry* magazine (1978), and a John Simon Guggenheim Memorial Fellowship in poetry (1977–78).